True woman

Gregor Golob

ISBN-10: 1463743955
ISBN-13: 978-1463743956

Dedication

Dedicated to all women, men and lovers who know what is the right person for her and him.

Contents

True recognition

George is looking for a single woman in the social network. After several searches of single women in the social network find single woman profile of Tania. Out of curiosity write her, would like to know more about her. After some initial mutual cognitive messages Tania write back to George questions.

Tania:

Hello, George. Today I saw a nightmare. And I do not want to sleep longer. Strange, but lately I began to see in my dreams, lots of terrible things. I do not even know what it is connected. I guess I was just tired from work. What do you think George, why I do not sleep?

I would be pleased to hear your opinions and advice. I've always been pleased to communicate with people. And I always try to adhere to advice, if they somehow agree with my thoughts. I see that your weekend went well! I'm glad for you. My weekend was great too. I've been walking since the weather was beautiful! Temperature remained at around 2-3 degrees below zero. Also, I went with my friends at the cafe. And then I went to my mother. And I came home a few hours ago. I love to dance. I think all people love to dance. But many hesitate to do so. George, How much time you're looking for the girl on the Internet? And why did you decide to learn this way? Perhaps you have a computer at home, if you can spend a lot of time on dating sites in search of the woman. Am I right? I have a computer in my apartment. And I'm glad that I have access to the Internet. Because I can communicate with you. I always thought that the Internet is something of a rubbish heap. But in the Internet you can find something worthwhile. For example, I met you. And now, my attitude to the internet has changed for the better. After all, it brings together millions of people around the world. George, I came across one more question. Do you live alone or with parents? Do you own a house? I bought a year ago the apartment. Since I am a young professional, I pay only half price of the apartment. And the other half paid by the state. I took a loan that will pay for my accommodation. And after 4 months I paid with my credit. But I have my own house separate from my family. Strange, but I've always aspired to independence. What do you think about this?

George:

Hello! About your nightmare. From my experiences, you (your brain), some think about these things. Better, you to think about the beautiful things that you want to do. If you are more interested in detail, it is best that you find a book about these things. What do you say? Yes, I have a computer at home. From curiosity I'm looking for a woman on the Internet. I can easily get to know women from around the world. I live with parents in the house. My wish for the future is to buy the house. For me, the best is that I am independent. What should be your ideal type of man? I wish telling you that I also working on my website. My website is http://www.socialmulti.com. I hope that you enjoy my website and you learn something new which your interests. Have a great day! George

Tania:

Hi George. I have a couple of hours ago, came home from work. My day today was bad. At work, the boss yelled at me. The thing is, I'm late for work. And my mood this morning was ruined. And all day I felt lousy. When I got home, I sat on the sofa and closed her eyes. I wanted to turn away from everyday problems. But then I decided to call my mom. My mom is the most wonderful mom in the world. She always understood me. And she often gave me good advice. My mom saw a lot in my life. She survived her husband's death, my father. She is now 58 years old. But she does not like to sit still. She often goes to his friends. So, I called my mom. She said she did not need to pay attention to such trifles. Do not be offended by the fact that the boss yelled at me. However, I myself knew it. And the words of my mother reassured me. You know, usually I always treat life positively. I can not long be angry at someone. My resentment disappears after a few minutes. But today the exception. I was angry for a long time for my boss, although I understand that I have myself to blame. After a conversation with my mom, I sat down at the computer. I'm glad that you wrote to me. How was your day? Hopefully better than me? Listen, I wrote you that I live in

Cheboksary. Did you read my letter? George, Tell me what did you do today. What's going to do tonight? I'm going to watch the film "Avatar". I've watched this movie. But today I wanted to revise it. I really liked the movie plot. The entire film is dramatic and romantic. Have you watched this movie? After all, he makes us think about such feelings as love, willingness to make sacrifices. Tell me, George, what you aspire to this life? On it I finish my letter and I am waiting for your answer.

George:

Hello! Here at me is almost a whole week of nice sunny weather. I spend much time on creating my website. If I have time at night I look what good movie on TV or PC. I have watched the movie Avatar. I was like it! I wonder if you already saw the movie with title Inception? An interesting movie from the perception of human reality. I aspire to this life, for to make a better world, and learn people to be smarter and wise. I want to know more about you, which things you like it? What colors do you like? What is your favorite color? Have you ever been in Europe, in which European countries? I am waiting for your letter. George

Tania:

Hi George. I recently came home. I am very tired! And how was your day? Something interesting has happened or not? You want to know what I like. Well, it takes a lot of space in the letter. But I will try to answer a multiple. Well, I rarely watch TV. I prefer to watch movies on my computer. I love the novelty box office, as in the old movies already know the end. And I want to film intriguing. From the literature, I prefer science fiction and classic novels. Interesting choice, is not it? But there is no accounting for tastes. From the music I prefer the classics in the orchestra. I also like listening to pop, disco. My favorite color is green, and blue. And yours? I've never been in other countries. Because of Russia is very difficult to leave. And it is very expensive. Well, let's not talk about sad. Today I had a great day! After work, I decided to walk a little. And I decided to walk around the Victory Square. In my town there is such a place. It's very beautiful. In the summer everything is covered with greenery, and in winter all the glitters is silver! Oh, I forgot her. So. I enjoy the time after work. And I saw my old classmates. I was very happy to see him, because it took many years! You can not even imagine what emotions overwhelmed us! That was unexpected! Meeting with classmates full of smiles and memories. I was having fun. And I plunged into nostalgia. Of course people changed over the years. But at the meeting, we are changing, remembering himself in his youth. We talked for a long time, sat in a cafe. It turned out that my classmates went to the north of Russia. And there they live rather well. I came home just now. Now already evening. And how are you? What did you do today? How long ago did you see your classmates? Well, I finish my letter and I am waiting for your answer. Bye! Until tomorrow!

George:

Hello! My day was held today in everyday normal day. My favorite color is blue, brown and silver. I'll go to Italy today. Italy is on the border with Slovenia, where I live. To Italy, I have a 3 km path. I have not a lot of time saw my classmates. I'm well. I wonder if you like to do something by hand, in terms of what to paint, fix, make some things by hand? Are you a morning person, make it difficult to get up in the morning?

If you had the opportunity, you to be awake all night until the morning with your favorite person? Waiting for your view on letter! George

Tania:

Hello, George. I am glad that I can see again your letter. I just went home and immediately checked my mail. For me, it has become like an attraction. Listen, I do not understand the end of your letter. You ask questions. But I do not understand their meaning. Can you explain ok?

I'm so easy to write to you, even though we know not very long. And I have a feeling that we are familiar with long, even though we know each other a few weeks. It is very interesting. What do you think, George? I never thought that I can easily communicate with someone from another country. And I do not care. Thanks to you I learned a lot, get used to you. And most importantly, I love it! You became for me something more than a friend. I can calmly entrust to you my secrets. I can communicate with you on any topic. And I wonder with you!

Did you ever have thought that you will communicate with the simple Russian girl who lives far away from you? If you had told me 4 years ago, that I will communicate with you, I would not have believed it. But now I realized that in life nothing is impossible. And this is very pleased with me. We have different languages, different mentality. But we are bound by something more. Can this friendship, maybe something big. George, Tell me what you think of me? I am very interested to know your opinion. Waiting for your answer. Until tomorrow!

George:

Hello! In view of my questions from the previous letter. I wonder if you rise up early in the morning? If you had the opportunity, you would have been awake all night until the early hours of morning with your favorite person? For me is interesting new to communicate with you in Russia. I think, you are sociable, simple, spontaneous, open mind, natural woman. Thank you for your trust in me. I did not imagine that I will be so easy to communicate with you. You like freedom? I like a lot of freedom. At the next moment! George

Tania:

Hello, my dear George. How are you today? You ask if I love freedom. But perhaps all love freedom. But total freedom is not and never will be. We will always be dependent on anything. Agree? As the weather in your town? In my city, the sky snow is falling. He walks in the morning. It seems that he wants to cover an entire city. And now I want to be this snow, I want to cover thee with my kisses. But the distance blocks do this to me. Today I went for a walk in the park. Strange, but I did not feel cold. I slowly walked along the snow-covered alley. Now very few people come to the park. And I was glad, because I can walk freely, I know that I will not be disturbed. I thought about you, about myself, about our lives. You know, I wonder sometimes walk and ponder life. Today I have a strange feeling. It feels like the inside of me is empty. Perhaps this is due to the fact that I am alone. Now I read your letter. My eyes glide along the lines of the letter. Your letter like a window into another world. If we had not met, I never would have learned about another life in another country, about you. When I first wrote you, I was a little scared and timid, but still interesting. I do not know what to write and how to start dating. But gradually my shyness disappeared. You became my very close friend. You agree with me, saying that we are more than friends? Friendship can exist only at the beginning when man and woman do not know each other well. I believe that our relationship with you moving in a new direction. Do you agree with me? You've written a lot about you. But I want to know you not only on your description. After all, the letters can not know the nature of man. Do you agree with me?

George:

Hello, I am glad today. Yes, we will always be dependent on anything. Today weather in my town is cloudy. Yes, we are more than a friends. And when, where do you want to meet with me? We'll have to agree on when, where and all other details that we meet in person. We will talk soon. George

Tania:

Hello my dear George. I am very pleased to receive your letter. How are you? What's your mood? I am pleased to see in my mailbox your letter. Listen, do you really want to meet? It seems to me that you do not want this. Too dry you write. So I do not want to risk it. Sorry. I want happiness. And you are scaring me. Tell me that you mean happiness? You want to be happy? Although this is probably a stupid question. On the Internet I found a description of happiness. This state of mind, consciousness. That's it! No one really can not define it. I believe that the person is happy when he understands and feels the happiness of every minute their lives. Yet no one was happy one day, week, month. Happiness - it's for life! Happiness - such a small word but it means so much! And for everyone in different ways! As for me ... Happiness - it's me, life, love, peace, environment, people, home, nature, moments, minutes, seconds, animals, sun, rain, night, day, the stars, the warmth, intimacy, what I'm doing, etc. But not all embrace it, so it's such a small word that is felt at the moment and at this moment ... or even now as I write, I'm happy that someone is interested in my thoughts! About happiness can talk endlessly ... Yes, it does not need to chase. and it is true, it is always in me, in you! Just feel it! Zoom it to yourself! Touch! And do not let go! Because - it is so instantly and slippery because of the wrong thoughts can escape! Do not allow this, that and the very trying! You must try to see it at all ... because it so much, but so few people notice it ... And it's sad. But lately, for me happiness is that you write to me. I understand that I'm not alone in this world that I'm interested. And I am now curious to know your opinion. What for you happiness? Maybe the family the children? Or something else?

George:

Hello! I am fine. How are you? I really want to meet you. For me happiness mean that I live by my beliefs and I realize my plans and desires. Also people, children, nature. I am a subscriber to email news from the areas of personal growth. I sending you the contents of the news that the last email I received. I hope you like the content. What do you think about this substance? Best reading!

7 Keys for Joyful Living!

Know your purpose. Nothing will bring you joy more than knowing what it is that you are about on this earth. Not knowing brings sadness, wondering, fear and lack of fulfillment. Above all, find out what your unique purpose is here on this earth - then fulfill it! As you do, you will experience joy!

Live purposefully. This is a follow up to number one. It is one thing to know your purpose, but then you need to live according to that purpose. This is a matter of priorities. Let your actions and schedule reflect your purpose. Don't react to circumstances and let them cause you to live without your purpose fully in sight. Living without your purpose will cause frustration. Living purposefully will bring you deep satisfaction and joy!

Stretch yourself. Don't settle into the status quo. That will leave you unfulfilled. Always look to stretch yourself. Whatever you are doing, stretch yourself to do more! Stretching yourself will break the limits you have set for yourself and will cause you to find joy in your expanded horizons!

Give more than you take. It brings happiness to accumulate. It brings joy to give away. Sure, getting the car you worked hard for will bring you a sense of satisfaction and even happiness. But it won't bring you joy. Giving something away to the less fortunate will bring you deep, abiding joy.

Surprise yourself, and others too. The words here are spontaneity and surprise! Every once in a while, do the unexpected. It will cause everybody to sit back and say, "Wow, where did that come from?" It will put a little joy in your life, and theirs.

Indulge yourself sometimes. Too much indulgence and you are caught in the happiness trap. Looking for the next purchase, celebration etc to bring you a little "happiness high". But if you will allow yourself an infrequent indulgence as a reward for a job well done and a life well lived, you will appreciate the indulgence and experience the joy of it.

Laugh a little - no, a lot! Most people are just too serious. We need to laugh a little - no, a lot! Learn to laugh daily, even if you have to learn to laugh in bad situations. This life is to be enjoyed! The next time you go to the movie rental store, get a comedy and let loose!

Let yourself laugh! Joy can be yours! Look for it, pursue it and enjoy it! George

Tania:

Hi, my teddy bear! How are you today? Honey, how was your day? I liked the news content. Well I will try to follow them. Hopefully I'll be happy. How was your mood during the day? I have a very good mood today. Long ago I was not so good. I love you and now all my thoughts only about you! You are forever captured my heart. I can not love anyone else except you! I will always give you my love and his tenderness! My love you are so dear to me that I was ready to give everything just to be with you! We will overcome the distance, we will overcome time and will be together! Tomorrow I'll talk to my boss about my vacation. As you look at it? I also consulted about the trip to your country. I learned that I can fly freely in your country. But it only needs to make a passport, visa and some documents. I know all the details tomorrow and write you all. I can not go on without you. I'm afraid that if we do not meet you in the near future, you can find and fall in love with another woman. I am very afraid of losing you. Cute write me please, what do you think about our meeting. You really want our meeting? Write me your thoughts. I dream to be with you. Your little princess Tania.

George:
Hi Tania! I am good today. Yes, I really want our meeting. About our meeting. Interestingly enough, will meet in person. What do you have to know about Europe? Bye, George

Tania:
Hello my dear George! How are you? Listen, why did you write so little? There is a feeling that you do not want a meeting. Look, I can change my mind and abandon the trip. It seems to me that you're not really are interested in our meeting. Or am I not right? "I hope that your letter will be great tomorrow . And is it something I should know about Europe, to go there? I think I know the geography. Hopefully, there will be problems? Today I talked with my boss about my vacation. I said that I was tired and I need a vacation. Fortunately, my boss saw me. And said that I can take a vacation for 2 months. What do you think about this? I

think it's wonderful! My boss travels every year to rest in Egypt. And he said that if I am going abroad, I shall use the services of a travel agency. My dear, I've asked my friends, in which the travel agency is better and faster to do the documents. My boss suggested that the most popular agency. After work I went to a travel agency to find out information about the trip. Yesterday I had imagined our meeting with you. I presented at the meeting as we hugged each other and gave a passionate kiss! My honey, it's wonderful that we will soon meet and be together. My love, when I went to a travel agency, for a while I just went and watched the names of the rooms. I do not know where I go to learn about the trip for you. In the end I got confused in the names of the rooms. So I decided that it would be better to ask someone. I went to the woman who sat on a chair and someone was waiting. The woman turned out to be quite amiable, she told me in a room I will need to go. I came into the office and went to one of the employees. I asked what do I need to travel to you. My dear George, he told me to go to your country first of all need a tourist visa, it must be done first. but this has to do a passport and medical insurance. And of course to purchase tickets. Besides all this have to do a lot of references. But this is the most basic that I should have so that I could fly to you. My love, travel agency, all it can do for me on short notice. If I make out without all the travel agency, it would take a very long time and a lot more money. And with the agency I will do everything necessary for our meeting. What do you think: this is wonderful? The agency explained to me that it will be much easier to make the documents through their agency. My love do you think? I sign a contract?

George:

Today, here at me is nice sunny weather. That you know more about my country I sending you website on Slovenia http://www.slovenia.info. I am interested in our meeting. I see that you like to write a lot and in detail. For me not the point that I write very much, I more like that things are done. I hope you understand. You do what you know is the best for you regarding travel to Slovenia and all other things. How did you go today day? Have a sucessfull day! George

Tania:

Good afternoon my love George. I am very glad to your reply to my letter ... How was your day? My honey, you learned something new about our meeting? Thank you for having sent a link to the site. I would be interested to explore Slovenia, while my documents and visas will be made. I learned that I should have to come to you. But I did not even ask the amount required to design a package of documents and booking tickets. My honey, today I did not have time to go to the agency. So I'm going there tomorrow. I hope that the cost would be within reasonable limits. But if I have problems? My honey, then what do I do? I can count on your support and help? It's our meeting, our first date in reality! You know, George, my heart happy that it is in the cradle of the most gentle of hands. My heart loves pure light, not exacting love. He does not need anything except the opportunity to be close to you, my dear George. And that I need ... to be near you, feel the warmth of your body, tenderness of your hands, feel your stupefying smell, melt in your arms, feel the taste of your kisses. I got a need for sleep and wake up with thoughts of you.

"Life is one. And you want to live it so as not to be excruciatingly painful for the wasted years." And I think this is the right word.

Love is omnipotent and boundless, its force does not depend on time of year, age, and technological progress. Heart meet - and flashes a sense, a beautiful, deep and inclusive, so it was and always will be ... My sweet, I love you! And I know that soon we'll be together! Waiting for your answer with impatience, my teddy bear! Kisses!

George:
Hello Tania! I am fine today. With me today is a beautiful sunny weather. I am glad that you are happy. What are you doing good today? Bye, George

Tania:
Hello my dear. How are you? How was your day? I could not write to you yesterday. I had to look after Inna. Lena was busy

and called me. I could not refuse. I hope you understand that? And my cousin is not available online at this time. So I could not warn you that I could not write on Saturday. I hope you're not offended, my teddy bear? I could not go to the agency today as it was closed. But tomorrow I'll write. OK? You know, days go for days. And my life does not change anything. It's so sad. I feel emptiness inside. And not just a void. This is a sucking void. I feel very lonely ... Every day I dream of escape from reality. But it fails me. I often think about my own life. And I do not see the point. Why suffer and suffer? I'm just want happiness. Is that so hard?!

George:
Hello! I am good. How are you? What are you doing today beautiful? I wish you a happy and creative days! George

Tania:
Hi George. I have a couple of hours ago, came home from work. Now, I quickly read your message. And I have a question after reading your letter. Do you even gonna talk to me? You know why I wrote? You just sent me a short message. I understand that you are now hard to write something. But if your next letter will be small, I remove them. I hope you understand? On it I finish my letter and I am waiting for your answer.

Tania:

Where have you gone?

Do not write, does not respond.

Not really an evil sorcerer

Pick you up baby!

Well! I caught him!

And eggs Blast off!

From the clutches of his nasty

I'll take you!

Or maybe fell out of love

In parting me?

And your passion has cooled

Without my fire?

Yes, this is not a problem

After all, I love thee!

When meeting a new force

I will kindle a fire in thee!

But if you're a traitor,

Spend the night with others!

And whisper it gently,

What is she such a one.

On this there is no forgiveness

At it is, goodbye!

Forever, my love

Weep and remember!

George:

Hello! How are you? I'm still here, you can write to me whenever you want. I had no time for you to answer. Sorry. Thanks for your poem. It is very beautiful. Have a creative day! George

Tania:

You have written a shorter letter. Again, a short letter !!!!!!! You write that apology. But can you forgive it? We talked about the meeting! And now you forgot about it ???!!! I'm tired of being alone. I'm going crazy from loneliness! I am sitting at home and once again I miss ... In my heart settled melancholy, my love George. And it is very difficult. Before that I had never experienced such a feeling ... And I now feel uncomfortable ... On the street, sunny day, but I did not enjoy it ... My George, I'm very bored. And I do not even know how to get rid of the boredom ... Now I added the music to somehow stifle spiritual emptiness ... But as luck would have heard the sad music that reminds me of you, George... My dear George, I feel like I'm lost! I really want to see you, be with you ... Every day I dream about our meeting ... I dream to be with you! But as time passes, but we also divided the distance ... I was very hurt, my love George ... And I want my pain is gone ...

Tania:

Hi! How are you? How is your day? Today is March 8. And today is International Women's Day! Is it in your country is not such a holiday? I thought you today to congratulate me on the holiday. I waited your letter. But my hopes were in vain. After all, you do not write! Of course I'm sad ... I thought you would find the time to congratulate me. But apparently now you have forgotten me. Perhaps you are now well rested? Well then, good luck! Take care!

George:

Hi, I am fine. Thank you for your affection to me. How are you a good soul? I'm still here. Yes, I could make written leter before. But I have not written before. They I want you to be happy where you are. Of which things you would like to talk about. Be you a good soul continues! George

Tania:

Hi! And may even say good night! Now it's too late in my town. But I do not want to sleep. So I decided to write to you. Are you awake? Or did you already see a beautiful dream? Tomorrow a day off! Oh, I'm waiting for it eagerly, because tomorrow I will again see my niece! I will walk with her and play! And what are you gonna do? Perhaps your weekend pass that wonderful? I'm guessing? Well I'm not going at night is very heavy on your head. Good night! Tania!

Tania:

Hi, my love, my George! How was your day? I hope that as well. In Russia the rainy weather and my bad mood. Only your letters warm me and make me smile and be happy that someone loves me (not counting my parents). I am very glad that you love me. In our world, it is very

difficult to find true love, but those who truly want to love, seeking its second half. So I found you, and you found me. As a child I dreamed of marrying a prince on a white horse. Then I loved to read romantic books, adventure stories and novels. I wanted my boyfriend was just as brave, caring, kind and strong like the heroes of novels. And then I met you. My whole life is turned upside down. I do not believe that really find love online. But now I am satisfied that the impossible is possible. How do I want to come to you and see you in reality and not in the photo. I want to feel the touch of your gentle hands on my face, I want to inhale the fragrance of your strong body, I want to feel the sweet taste of your tender lips. I love you and keep dreaming about our meeting. I dream about how I'm going off the plane and you meet me, I dream about how our bodies merge in a gentle hug! My dear George. You know perfectly well how close we are to each other, but at the same time, we shared a great distance ... Sweet I think that now is the time to reduce this distance and unite our hearts, our souls unite, unite our destinies. Are you ready for this? You want it? Very difficult for me to realize that my favorite so far away from me! Do you really want the same what I see? I can not wait for your answer!

George:
Hi Tania, Thank you for your sincerity and trust in me. My day is good. Yes, I wish personally talk to you about us two. How is went your day? Did anyone ever say that you have a gift for writing your letter are very high quality and full of inspiration! I wish you much joy. Thank you for your night star, George

Tania:
Hello My love George. What is your mood? My love George, I'm glad to see your new letter. My love, you know yourself, as I like getting a letter from you. In each letter I write to you, I want to say much about my feelings for you that sometimes I even write them for you until nightfall. But I sometimes difficult to express all my thoughts, feelings and ideas in a letter, even if it is large. They can only pass in reality. I love you! As a day? I'm very bored and sad, because I'm away from you. Probably my letter, where there are thousands of words that I write to you to replace one phrase "I love you George". but I want you to know how much I love you, how deep my love for you. Now I try to express in your letter, how deep my feelings for you and how much I

love you. I know that the letter can not convey all the love I feel for you. but I want you to understand my love for you. My love George, my love to you like a waterfall: The same strong. and it will flow and live forever. Our love gives life to us, and we can not live peacefully without her. Without love we feel thirsty, but if we love, we are pleased and happy. My love George, you agree with me? My love, my love for you is so strong that it permeates every cell of my body, and she gives birth. and I can enjoy every day. But I miss the love around you. My love George, you understand that? My dear, love is beautiful when two loving hearts together, together forever, because they love each other. My honey George, you want to be with me once and for all? My dear George, my love for you is like fire. She is as warm and glowing. It warms the cold evenings and gives us the strength to live. Without fire man can not live like I can not live peacefully without our love, because I love you very much. The fire, just like love is warm and gentle, but sometimes it is bright and glowing with passion. My love George, now my love for you is warm and gentle, and when we meet again, my love for you flamed and will become brighter with passion than they do now, because we will be together. We need to do the last step and we'll meet in reality! My honey George, now you understand how we need our meeting? My love George, we are very much in love and I want our love was "stormy river" and "passionate flames of fire". Do you want? I'll wait for a response ...

George:

Hello Tania, Joy is in the air. Tania are one passionate woman! You agree? Yes, I want be with you, with your thought. I sending you an interesting text. Enjoy in your reading! With a desire to become an Extraordinary Leader:

Continually pursue personal and professional growth,

Treating everyone I come in contact with the dignity and respect they deserve,

Finding the way for as many people as possible to benefit from my decisions and actions,

Be willing to make and carry out hard decisions without regard to personal expediency,

The highest level of personal and corporate integrity,

Tell the truth and be honest, regardless of potential personal loss,

Think "team" first,

Finding a person who can mentor me,

Finding at least one person I can personally mentor,

Help others discover their strengths and function in them,

Maintain my priorities and organize my life and work according to them,

Live a life of balance between work, family, and leisure,

Pursue balanced growth in body, soul and spirit - understanding that each area affects the others innately,

Pursue what is best - for myself, my organization, and for others - and not settle for that which is simply "good enough",

Do work and live a life that leaves behind a lasting legacy of excellence,

Build a team to surround me in order to enhance my strengths and make up for my weaknesses,

Surround myself with people who will tell me the truth and not just what they think I want to hear,

Become a great listener,

Be an Extraordinary Follower of those who are my leaders,

Help others develop their skills,

Dream big dreams and encourage others to do the same,

Stretch my followers enough to make them grow but not so much as to discourage them,

Be driven by vision, mission and purpose, not by circumstances or expediency,

View the world through optimistic eyes,

Embrace the concept of change as a positive force for improvement,

Be responsible in my actions as they relate to my commitments to myself and others,

Be tenacious in my pursuits,

Give more than I receive and to be characterized by generosity,

Show courage in the face of challenge,

Be an example of dedication and commitment,

Share the privileges of leadership with those who follow me,

Give power away to those who can share in it responsibly and help the organization,

Use both my head and my heart when leading,

Manage my time according to my priorities,

Be the first to sacrifice when sacrifice is needed,

Make all short-term decisions with the long-term goals in mind,

Develop a successor,

Develop excellent communication skills,

Use a variety of means of influence,

Be the primary strategy setter for the organization,

Teach others,

Inspire others,

Keep my eye on the big picture,

Making the complex simple,

Motivate others,

Consider others as important as myself,

Identify future leaders,

Train and develop future leaders,

Regularly reward accomplishment,

Allow followers to fail in their attempts at growth and innovation,

Work leadership development into every level of the organization,

Have a clear vision,

Remain calm in difficult situations,

Keep a sense of humor,

Remove people from their position as soon as I know they need to go,

Empathize with others.

I hope you will! George

Tania:

Hello my love George!!! How are you my prince??

I'm glad your new letter. But why did you sent me a text which is written how to become a leader? Why do I need it?! Or you just do not want to answer my questions and posted it? But why do not you answer my questions? Of course it saddened me. Why do you deal thus with me?? After all, I have no man more beautiful and more important than you are my prince! Only with you I'm so nice and sweet. You have become my main part of life, especially what could be more in life and always be near. My love for my life was divided into two intervals. First, when I knew you when my life was sad and lonely, and the second after an acquaintance with you my sweet! I'm so happy and glad for me to get such a wonderful and joyous time. But I'm still alone. The only thing that when you write to me, it brings me pleasure. My love I want something else that has not been with us ever dream about all the lovers. But is there between us this feeling?

George:

Hello Tania! Are you full of surprises. Thank you for your nice words and thoughts! Nature is awakening. Look at the starry sky. First you see a star, then I think of you! I did not think that you'll so much affection for me. I am glad that you are what you are. Love for you. George

Tania:

Hi George! How are you? Do you have decided to answer me? Where have you been so long? And will you continue to lose? And how was your weekend? My weekend went pretty well. Although I was just sitting at home. Although not. I went to the store and bought yogurt. I love to drink yogurt! This is a tasty and healthy. And then I spent the whole evening sitting at home and watched TV. Actually, I do not like watching TV. But yesterday I did not want to walk. Because the street is damp! Still, there is the approach of spring. To the same and my internet is cut off yesterday afternoon. And he has appeared only today. Well this is my letter to a close. I'll wait for your answer. Take care!

Tania:

Hello, my dear George. How are you? How was your day? I hope that as well. You ask what I love to drink and eat. What a strange question. Well, I love pizza and tea. Of course I eat and other dishes. But I wrote you my favorite. By the way, I'm still really, really love ice cream! You know, I'm going tonight to go to the cinema for the session. But in the last minute, I abandoned this idea. I do not want a film look. I do not want to wake up each day alone in a cold bed! I do not want to live alone! It is a pity that we are now separated by distance. My sweet, we are adults who have the right to love, happiness. We are now communicating via the Internet. But we can not always communicate well and to write letters to one another. We must be more serious. Do you agree with me? And I got the idea for a meeting. Of course I used to think about it. But then it seemed something funny and frightening. But now I think that the real meeting, we can live show each other our feelings. Yes, I am afraid of the distance. But I love you! And I think that distance is nothing, only a small obstacle. And if we want, then quietly overcome this obstacle. What do you think about it, my angel? Is it real? After one meeting will replace the many days of communication on the Internet! I'm right, my sweet? This issue, I finish my letter. And now I'm waiting for your answer. Kiss!!!!

George:
Hello Tania! Today at me is beautiful sunny day. I agree with you on one meeting will replace the many days of communication on the Internet. I wonder if you have a facebook account? Something interesting is happening in your city? Thank you Tania! George

Tania:
Hello, my George! I am very glad to your letter ... How are you doing? How mood? I see that you agree that the meeting will replace the many conversations on the Internet. But I wrote to

you that I shall have to fly to you. Remember? And what do you say? And by the way, I do not have access to facebook now! I forgot the password, the new profile I do not want to create! I want to share with you my thoughts: One day, while walking, I stopped for a moment and thought about many things, which I do not. But suddenly I realized that I have you and felt whole and happy person! I really missed you, my sweet, you yourself just can not imagine. Very, very, very strongly. When will it all end? I'm dying in this hell without you. I'm just dying. Not nice to me, white light. And this expectation, infinitely stretching minutes.

I look out into the street - a fabulously beautiful sky, stars like thousands of lit together lights, new moon, silence, the soft light of lanterns everything looks special. But without you. Is this true? When your heart is truly great, it seems that almost feel it, so it is full of love. When suddenly want to talk, to tell you all that I feel. And again, nothing, you seem so elusive. Why are you there? Just want to cuddle up to you, feel your power, feel so fragile in your strong arms, simply dissolve. Think, just a naive girl with a childish romantic vision of the world? No, I just love you ... And on this my email is nearing an end. Take care my angel! I'm waiting for a response from you! Kiss!

George:
Hello Tania! I am glad today. How go your day? For your fly to me. When you dare to come to me I'll wait you. Thank you Tania for your love to me. George

Tania:

I'm not sad, I just miss you ...

As winter sun to light summer jet

As a cup of jasmine tea tart

Misses out on your lips, remembering the kiss ...

As the clouds miss the dawn,

As the rain at the Rainbow magic in the sky

As a muse for the poet in love,

As luck women sparks in the eyes of ...

I'm not sad, I just yearn for you ...

As the star of the Milky Way,

How butterfly wings in the wind kisses

As the heart yearns for love locked up ...

Rains separations, and will be the sun - I know!

And a rainbow of happiness will swing in the clouds ...

In the meantime ... I still miss you ...

The taste of chocolate on your lips ...

George:

Hello Tania! A poet, a romantic soul Tania. How go your day?
Thank you for your poetry. You write a lot of time poetry? It is a
very original writing your poetry. I like your poetry! George

Tania:

Hello my angel! How are you today? I am very pleased that you liked my poem. By the way, why do not you wrote a few days? Do you even got my letter on March 26? After all, I wrote to you: Hello my love George!!!! How is your mood today? My sweet I am sad again! But I know that soon we can be together! Today I went to a travel agency. My dear the travel agency told me that I will have to pay around 450 euros for the documents that I have no problem could come to your country and stay in it. I will eagerly wait for your answer.

Tania:

Hello my angel George! You know, I'm angry at you. The feeling that you did not think of me! I'm waiting like a fool for your letter! I like a fool to believe that we will meet! But you can not even write me a letter! Apparently you can not put you on my space! But I am angry, but my heart is very, very excited! Suddenly happened to you that something bad ??!!!! And I do not know anything and am in the dark! Write me as soon as possible. I'll be waiting! I love you my angel!!!! Your Tania!

Tania:

Hi, again missing an angel! How was your weekend?. I hope it's great! On weekends I sleep a lot! I guess I have a spring depression. I do not want to do anything! And I have briefly gone online. But this is a very common problem in my town. Internet access is very, very bad. Now I sit at the computer. On the street the night! And I want to see your letter! Kiss! Tania!

George:

Hi Tania! How are good hearts princess? I'm still here. I had a great weekend. I'm went to dance for the weekend. In view of our meeting. Yes it would be very nice to meet in person and to be together to talk. Of which things you would like yet to talk about? Best!

Tania:

Hello my love George. How do you feel loved? Again I checked my mailbox. As soon as I saw your letter, I am very glad that you did not forget me! You write that it would be nice to meet. My happiness, our love is not without compare. My heart has a lot of love, and I am ready to give you a heart that you know how much much I love you. My angel George, I am pleased that I love you. I'm sure we'll be able to be together soon. My dear George, I have every letter you write, that I love you. I am writing this so that our feelings are not dead. Only if we're going to write that we love each other, between us will never extinguish the flame of love. My favorite George, I very much want you to be too in your every letter he wrote to me that you love me, how much you love me. My love George, because I was one very hard to maintain our love. My prince, tell me honestly you'll be able to help our meeting? George I no longer have hope in anyone. Only your Tania.

Tania:

Hello my angel George! You're still a long time will make me wait for your letter? Why do you always make me worry?! Are not you ashamed? If we decide to meet, why you so carelessly relate to this? Or you've already got sick girlfriend? Or are you so much busy that you have no opportunity to get 5 minutes of free time to write me a letter to reassure me?? Lately I do not understand you! And I'm starting to be disappointed! You treat me like a baby! And I'm hurt and want to cry, you're so little time given to me! I have no words! Waiting for your reply as soon as possible! Tania.

Tania:

Hi dear! How are you? What you will do today, in Friday? And when you write me? I MISS YOU SO MUCH!!

George:

Hello Tania! I am fine today on friday. I'll go a little with the bike today. What say glad TANIA today? Have a sunny beautiful day!

George:

Hi Tania! How are Tania? I wish you a glad, happy your birthday. Do today something special what you want for your birthday! HAVE fun!!!!!!!!!!!!!! George

Tania:

Thanks for the birthday greetings. This is slightly improved my mood. Yesterday I said my birthday is pretty sad. I called to visit my cousin, my niece and my mother. And the four of us sat up late at night. Basically we talked about our plight. But it's better than nothing. By the way, you're lost again for a long time. Why do you treat me so? If you started talking to me, then do not disappear! Uncomfortable every time to write and ask where you're missing! Are you lost all conscience ??!!!

Tania:

Good morning George! I decided to write you this morning because I want to make my cheerful and happy mood to tell you! Today I dreamed that I was on top of the Himalayas and look down. Veeeeeeeeeeeeery beautiful!!!!!!!!! It is a pity that it was only a dream. But even after I woke up, I still feel that the charm and beauty! And I wanted to share it with you! And what you saw in a dream? And what are your plans for today? And what about our meeting? I do not know what to think! I will wait for your answer! Once again, good morning! Tania!

George:

Hi Tania! Very nice dream you had. Thank you for share your dream with me. I plan for today to go cycling. Good day!

Tania:

Hello, my dear George! I am very glad that you wrote ... George I love you! Are you planning to cycling? Great! My love for you has become even stronger! I'm constantly thinking about you, wanted to be with you ... In my dreams often were you ... By the way, why do not you write anything about a meeting? So we meet or not! My dear George, when you're asleep, then you have encountered the feeling when you realize that you're in a dream? This is wonderful! Yesterday I was asleep. And suddenly I realized that I'm in a dream ... And I flew off to you! But when I almost flew to thee, on my way got some sort of invisible barrier. And I could not fly to you! I'm very disappointed ... And then I woke up. My dear George, for my eyes were full of tears ... Apparently, I was crying in his sleep. Perhaps it's because I was not able to overcome an obstacle ... We're also unable to meet in reality. And because of this I suffer even more ... My love George, tell me when we're together? Is it very difficult? I can not come to you. Why travel costs so much??

Tania:

Good good morning, honey! Enough to yawn, smile little angel! Get up, stretch, fending off sleep and laziness! And let the joy be today! let my words will warm you in the early hour, Morning sun will smile, cheer us up! Know that you remember and miss you very much! I can not live without you the day or night!

George:
Hello Tania! How are you? Thank you for your nice thoughts for me! Have a great day and night! George

Tania:
Hello, my dear George, my love. I really missed you. At the weekend I went to my mother. Since it is very pleasant to talk. My mom always understand me, always support them. And she always scolds me because I'm still not married. But I always reassure her by saying that I have everything in front. Love - like many in this word to my heart, merged ... I do not know where she is, I do not know who she is, but I know it just is ... We know about each other, we know what we are and what we meant for each other. Simply, we have not met yet ... But I love ... And I know that he loves ... The day will come and the hour when our hearts meet ... And then all the words of love, which over the years accumulated an involuntary separation within us, we will explain to each other, and overflowing with unbridled passion, rinemsya into endless expanses of our senses ... In the end, love is not to look at each other, and to look in one direction. But when it happens? When we meet again my angel! And I want to finish my letter with the singer Victor Tsoy: Love, gentlemen, in

the same direction, do not let yourself and others like left and right. One life, and love - even more so.

And:

Death is worth living,

Love is worth the wait ...

George:

Hello Tania! Thank you for your sincerity to me. It's nice to read your thoughts. Maybe it is good for you to go out on weekends to party and meet new people, friends women and men. What do you say? Good luck for the future of your path. Sunny day for you! George

Tania:

Hello dear George, How are you? Thank you for your letter. But it was not pleased me ... But I feel bad that we are far away. We write to for a long time, but the real action to meet there. What to do? Correspondence for a month, a year? If the point? If we meet, there is no point in our correspondence ... Our feelings will die. You're an adult man and understands everything.

It hurts me to say this, but if in the near future, we will not meet, the better for us to part. Do you know why I say that? Because the letters do not reduce the distance that is between us. Understand. I have no money to come to you. My friends and parents, too, no money ... And you do not write anything at all for help ... I love you, but it hurts me to think that we are far from each other. I ask you, dear about the meeting, but you answer vaguely or completely ignoring my questions. One gets the impression that you play with me and kidding me. I am not a toy, I am a woman who wants to love and be loved. Do you understand me? After this letter, can you give me not to write or tell me all about the meeting. I want to hear the whole truth. I hope that you are an honest man, and answer all my questions. Waiting for your answer dear George. Your Tania.

George:

Hello Tania! I am very good. How go your day? I see that you'd like to look to true love. I at this moment I can not meet with you. I have commitments and errands. Maybe we'll meet in the future. I know you are a good soul, so I wish you to meet the person who will take from you the right loved woman. Perhaps it is true that you meet another loved man, I am in this moment I can not be physically present with you. What do you say good soul? See the good things in people. Thank you for be Tania, Your George

Tania:

Hey why do you continue to write to me if we can not meet now ??!!! Understand, I do not want to have friends on the Internet. I think this is stupid ... I'm looking for a serious relationship because I am lonely. and you just torment my heart. I'm sorry, but do not write me anymore. Good day for you!

George:

Hello! How are you Tania? Did you watch the Royal wedding? I liked the bride dress. What do you say? Best day and weekend! George

Tania:

Oh, you're still writing to me. Well I'm glad you're still writing to me. Why did not you answer me before? What is the cause of your grievance? Because if you did not write to me, then you take offense at me. But I wonder what I let you down? I hope this is not serious? Well, how are you? What did you do? Perhaps you found a girl in your country? I'm kidding! I'm reminded why we stopped talking. I ask you for help because she could not pay for the trip. Right? And you do not want to help me. And I think that's why I wrote you again? And why did you answer me? Is between us all over? What do you think? Waiting for your answer.

P.S. I have not watched Royal wedding. And there was that interesting? Can the Internet have video? Can you find me?

George:

Hello Tania! I am good. I thought that you do not want more to writes with me. I am not yet found my girl. You found your Romeo? For me, between us is still all open for the best friendship ... I have a lot to do. I am looking for a woman like you. For Royal wedding link at http://www.bbc.co.uk/news/uk-11767495. Wating for your answer. George

About the author

Gregor Golob was born in Slovenia, Europe. He is a 32 years old freelance book writer.

Thanks for the chose my book True woman. Enjoy the reading!

Gregor Golob